D1379500

A PICTURE BOOK OF ANCIENT BRITISH ART

A PICTURE BOOK
OF
ANCIENT BRITISH ART

BY

STUART PIGGOTT

Abercromby Professor of Prehistoric Archaeology
in the University of Edinburgh

AND

GLYN E. DANIEL

Fellow of St John's College and Lecturer in Archaeology
in the University of Cambridge

CAMBRIDGE
AT THE UNIVERSITY PRESS
1951

PUBLISHED BY
THE SYNDICS OF THE CAMBRIDGE UNIVERSITY PRESS
London Office: Bentley House, N.W. 1
American Branch: New York
Agents for Canada, India, and Pakistan: Macmillan

Printed in Great Britain at the University Press, Cambridge
(Brooke Crutchley, University Printer)

CONTENTS

CONTENTS

PREFACE

Most introductory books on the prehistory of the British Isles, and more especially the moderately priced ones, are unable to include, from the nature of things, more than a few illustrations of the art of the varied peoples who inhabited these islands in the many centuries that stretch back from the Roman conquest to the first appearance of man in north-western Europe, some three-quarters of a million years ago, according to the reliable calculations of the geochronologists. The illustrations that appear in such books have to show, in any case, not only the artistic achievement of early man, but those aspects of his culture in which what is usually called art is not very evident—houses and tombs, fields, farms, tools and workshops. We count ourselves therefore fortunate in having secured the co-operation of the Syndics of the Cambridge University Press in the production of this moderately priced book of pictures which is exactly what its title suggests—a collection of photographs illustrating the artistic achievements of the pre-Roman inhabitants of the British Isles.

It is inevitable that in the selection of pictures of works of art there should be plenty of room for individual judgement, prejudice and taste. One aspect of the artistic achievement of early man we have excluded from our collection, namely architecture: the reader will not find here photographs of Lanyon Quoit, New Grange, Stonehenge, Skara Brae, Chysauster, or the Broch of Mousa. The architecture of prehistoric Britain would fill another book like this: indeed, of making collections of pictures like these there could be no end. What we have done is to produce a selection; we have been surprised to find that we agreed on the selection ourselves. We do not expect our colleagues to agree with our selection—because it is not theirs; but we have tried to make it representative and at the same time to include those things which are both pleasing to us to-day as well as the best of certain schools of art in the prehistoric past. Our aim has been twofold—to provide the serious student of early Britain with a short but representative collection of ancient British art, and to reveal to the general reader who may pick up this book that the art history of Britain does not begin, as so many still think, with the Lindisfarne Gospels and the Alfred Jewel. We have a heritage of British art which goes back, in a vigorous and varied form, to 2000 B.C. and, in isolated examples, even further.

But we do not want readers to regard this book as yet another introduction to the study of pre-Roman Britain. These objects should be viewed—and it is our earnest hope that seeing them in these pages will inspire many to view the real things in our national and local museums—not because they are old, but because many of them are of supreme beauty and a part of the heritage of the British spirit. Professor R. E. M. Wheeler has described the design of the Trawsfynydd tankard handle (no. 73) as ranking 'amongst the highest achievements of one of the most brilliant phases in the history of purely decorative art', and in the same way we think it no false archaeological snobbery to speak of the Birdlip mirror (no. 41) as superb in craftsmanship and perfect in its artistic achievement. It may be a mistake in many cases to study the art of a period apart from its history and social conditions, but we think it valuable occasionally to see things such as those in the following plates apart from their contexts—the archaeological industries and sites which so many people, genuinely interested in pre-Roman Britain, find difficult to understand. We then have a chance to appreciate them by independent standards of aesthetic satisfaction. Realization of these difficulties has also led us to give in each instance a date in years to the work of art illustrated, even if approximate within a century or two. Here again we are open to criticism, but we have felt that, however provisional, such dates were essential to the ordinary reader and not really confusing to the specialist.

As the pictures are the main purpose of the book, we have confined the letterpress to a short introduction, and a catalogue giving details of provenance, scale, material, etc., in addition to general comments on each piece.

Our thanks are due to the following who have assisted us in our search for good photographs and in the preparation of this little book:

Mr J. W. Brailsford, of the British Museum,
Mrs E. M. Clifford,
Professor E. Estyn Evans, of Queen's University, Belfast,
Sir Cyril Fox,
Professor S. P. ÓRíordáin, of the National University, Dublin,
Dr Joseph Raftery, of the National Museum of Ireland, and
Dr H. Savory, of the National Museum of Wales;

and to the following for supplying photographs and permission to reproduce objects in their collections:

PREFACE

The British Museum (1, 10–15, 27, 36–7, 47–9, 53–9, 62–7, 70–2)

The National Museum of Wales, Cardiff (28–9, 34–5, 42, 51–2)

The National Museum of Antiquities, Edinburgh (8, 9, 16, 18, 25, 33, 38–40, 61)

The National Museum of Ireland, Dublin (17, 21–4, 31, 34–5, 45)

The Museum of Archaeology and Ethnology, Cambridge (5–7, 19, 20, 26, 50)

The Hull Museum (30)

The Colchester and Essex Museum (32)

The Gloucester Museum (41)

The Torquay Museum (68–9)

The Liverpool Museum (73)

The Ashmolean Museum (60; Major Allen's photograph)

Colonel J. C. Wynne-Finch (51–2)

Mrs Dent-Brocklehurst (44)

The Duke of Northumberland (46)

Mrs Thomas H. Mason of Dublin (2–4)

Mr R. J. C. Atkinson (61), and

The Central Office of Information (38–40).

S.P.
G.E.D.

December, 1950

INTRODUCTORY ESSAY

We have called this book *A Picture Book of Ancient British Art* advisedly, because it consists of selected examples of the art of those people who lived in the British Islands in ancient times. The phrases 'ancient Britain' and 'ancient British' are somehow not very much used at the present day: they have been replaced by such terms as 'prehistory' and 'prehistoric archaeology'. This may be in part due to changing fashions in nomenclature, but also, perhaps, because they savour of those ancient Britons, the woad-painted chariot-driving savages described by Caesar, who formed the curtain-raisers of most standard histories of Britain until very recently. In the days when the only sources for the early history of Britain were literary, the most that could be hoped for was a threefold division into ancient Britons, Romans and Saxons.[1]

The development of prehistoric archaeology in the last hundred years and more has provided an entirely different background against which to view the ancient British—one now based on the material used mainly in the manufacture of tools and weapons. This framework, which began in the early nineteenth century with a recognition that in the prehistoric past man went through three successive stages of industrial development which were called the Stone Age, the Bronze Age, and the Iron Age, has since been elaborated and subdivided, and now provides at best a rough-and-ready guide to the dating of prehistoric objects. But this nomenclature still has general recognition, so that we must view the development of prehistoric art, illustrated here, against this background. We give below a table of these subdivisions together with their approximate dates, with reference to southern Britain at least. The table works from the bottom upwards:

Early Iron Age (*A*, *B* and *C*)	from 450 B.C. to A.D. 43.
Late Bronze Age	from 1000 B.C. to 450 B.C.
Middle Bronze Age	from 1500 B.C. to 1000 B.C.
Early Bronze Age	from 1700 B.C. to 1500 B.C.
Neolithic or New Stone Age	from 2000 B.C. to 1700 B.C.
Mesolithic Age	from 8000 B.C. to 2000 B.C.
Upper Palaeolithic Age	from 20,000–25,000 B.C., say, to 8000 B.C.

[1] See T. D. Kendrick's study, *British Antiquity* (1950).

Lower and Middle Palaeolithic Age	from the first appearance of man in southern Britain, perhaps 750,000 years ago, to 20,000–25,000 B.C.

These dates are only a general guide; in any case very exact dates are not possible in prehistory. But even in the later stages of prehistory in Britain, that is to say, in the last 2000 years B.C. when more exact chronology is possible, the various phases of the industrial stages must be understood as varying from place to place. Thus the absolute dates of each stage vary from one part of the British Isles to another; and while the people in south-east England were in the Early Iron Age, communities in Wales and Ireland were still in the Late Bronze Age.[1]

The subdivisions of prehistory based on the technological development of man, while they are still convenient as a guide to the ancient art of Britain, mask a more important subdivision of man's prehistoric culture which is of great significance in the development of art. From the point of view of art we can discount the Lower and Middle Palaeolithic Ages, from which no art has survived unless we include the beautifully chipped hand-axes of flint and hard-grained rocks. The hunters, fishers and gatherers of roots and berries who lived in the British Isles before the last great advance of the Pleistocene ice-sheet, had no art, and the same is true for western Europe and the world as a whole. The birth of art dates from the Upper Palaeolithic period, and the first artists were the Upper Palaeolithic hunters and fishers who flourished at the end of the last great glaciation and whose societies the archaeologist has labelled by such names as Aurignacian, Perigordian, Solutrean and Magdalenian, according to different assemblages of tools. Everyone has heard of the art of these Upper Palaeolithic folk, who carved and engraved objects of bone and stone, and who painted and engraved naturalistic animal designs in such caves of southern France and northern Spain as Font de Gaume, Combarelles, Lascaux, and Altamira.

The first stage of western European art history is, then, the Upper Palaeolithic, and the first stage of ancient British art includes the impoverished representatives of this great art cycle found in Britain, at that time very much the *ultima Thule* of prehistoric Europe. The British Isles have no examples of the magnificent cave art of the Upper Palaeolithic artists of south France and

---

[1] For a general account of pre-Roman Britain see J. Hawkes, *Early Britain* (1945), Hawkes and Hawkes, *Prehistoric Britain* (1947), J. G. D. Clark, *Prehistoric England* (1940), S. Piggott, *British Prehistory* (1950), and Childe, *The Prehistoric Communities of the British Isles* (1940).

north Spain, but it provides a few poor examples of decoration on portable objects. The group of hunters and fishers labelled the Creswellians by archaeologists lived in the rock shelters of the Derbyshire hills at the end of the last ice age; they were cousins of the Aurignacians and Magdalenians of France. One of their designs, the masked man engraved on a piece of bone, opens our display of ancient British art (no. 1): it could perhaps be dated somewhere between 10,000 and 15,000 years ago.

The hunters and fishers who succeeded the Upper Palaeolithic societies, and who go by the archaeological label of Mesolithic, lived in Britain from the end of the ice age to about 2000 B.C. While the Mesolithic folk of other parts of Europe had an art of great interest,[1] there is little from Britain to be placed in this phase. The real art history of early Britain begins round about 2000 B.C., when the first peasant village communities are found. These communities, at first formally Neolithic, and many of them soon metal-using, provide us with our first picture of a native British school of art. Of course in the study of prehistoric art one is very conscious of the limitations of prehistory caused by the differential survival of differing substances. The disappearance of paint may have altered completely our view of some phases (just as it has our view of the stone carvings of the Middle Ages and later centuries), while decoration on wood only rarely survives; for example, the wooden shield (nos. 23, 24), and the model figures (nos. 30–33). Thus it is that most of the objects here portrayed are of stone, bone, gold, bronze, or pottery.

Another of the limitations of prehistory, which becomes apparent as the following pages are turned over, is that in very many cases we have no certain knowledge of the purpose of the objects concerned. The purpose of the Irish bronze bowls or disks (nos. 48, 49) and the Llyn Cerrig crescentic bronze plaque (no. 42), for example, is very much in doubt, and so is the purpose of the Folkton chalk objects (nos. 12–15) and of such things as the Lattoon disk (no. 22). The small carved chalk objects from Folkton are probably best understood as idols; their decoration includes the curious stylized face motif which appears on similar cylindrical objects in south Spain, on collective tombs in France, and is widespread in the prehistoric Mediterranean. It may represent the Earth-Mother goddess whose cult was so ubiquitous in pre-historic times in that area. Whatever they were, they emphasize that the symbolism of prehistoric art must in most cases escape us, and that most of

---

[1] See particularly J. G. D. Clark, *The Mesolithic Settlement of Northern Europe* (1936), chapter IV.

1-2

the time we have to be content with recording the designs and forms that were adopted.

But while in some respects the study of prehistoric British art suffers from all the limitations of prehistoric scholarship, in others it transcends them as do few other aspects of prehistoric study. We can feel a kinship with the artists who made the Fordham beaker (nos. 5, 6), the Chippenham axe-hammer (no. 19) and the Dunaverney shaft-mounting (no. 36), for example, which is denied to us when we consider their economy and burial customs. And the results of contemplating the original appearance of some of the things illustrated here—the Mold horse-armour shining on the breast of a small Welsh pony (no. 27), the Torrs horse-mask (nos. 38–40) and the object from Deskford (no. 61) brought out on ceremonial parades, the bright enamels shining on the La Tène armour and trappings—are in strange contrast to many of the reflexions on prehistoric man prompted by the excavation of rubbish pits and graves. As Mr de Navarro has said elsewhere, 'it is amazing to think of how these artists, living amid the squalor, stink and barbarism of Iron Age surroundings, could attain the highly sophisticated simplicity of such works'.[1]

The objects and designs shown here, excluding the one example of Palaeolithic art (no. 1), can be divided roughly into three groups: the first representing the art of the first peasant village communities of, very roughly, the second millennium B.C., the period of the archaeological divisions, Neolithic, Early Bronze Age and Middle Bronze Age (nos. 2–20); the second group representing the art of the first two-thirds of the first millennium B.C., that is, the archaeological periods, Late Bronze Age and Hallstatt (or, in Britain, Iron Age *A*) (nos. 21–36); and thirdly, the art of the Celtic artists in Britain, from the third century B.C. to the first century A.D., Iron Age *B* and *C* (nos. 37–73). But it must be stressed that though these three groups may be so distinguished here, they are, except for the third, the Celtic art group, no more than a convenience for discussion. There was no unity in the art of Britain in the second millennium; we can distinguish neither a constant development, nor schools and trends. But in the third group there is an underlying unity of style, with a consistent development and various local traditions, like the north-eastern English school (nos. 38–40, 46, 47, 59) and the south-western school (nos. 41, 44).

In our first group we may, without postulating any underlying connexions, observe two clear traditions in the art. The first is the tradition of rectilinear

[1] Knowles and Charlesworth, *The Heritage of Early Britain* (1951).

4

geometrical ornament which appears in the chevrons, lozenges and bands of the beakers (nos. 5–7), of the Kilmartin bowl (nos. 8, 9), of the Poltalloch jet necklace (no. 16) and of the Irish *lunula* (no. 17). It is a simple tradition which probably springs from the Early Bronze Age communities of central Europe. The second tradition is one which appears on the walls of the great collective tombs, the megaliths and dolmens of popular parlance (see nos. 2–4), on the Folkton idols (nos. 12–15) and also on at least one of the carved balls (no. 18); it is what we may refer to, for want of a better word, as Megalithic art, and it contains spirals and geometrical figures of an entirely different tradition from those of the beakers and the metal work, as well as stylized versions of a human figure almost certainly to be connected with the Earth-Mother goddess of the Mediterranean. The culture of Britain in the second millennium B.C. is very much a blending of central European and Mediterranean elements and it is not surprising to find these two cultural provinces reflected in the art.

In making any general survey of British art of the second and early first millennium B.C., therefore, it is convenient to discuss its application to the various substances in use during the Bronze Age for use or adornment. The patient grinding and polishing of stone could on occasion produce ceremonial pieces, such as the axe-hammer (no. 19) and the jadeite axe-head (no. 20), which give to a modern mind something of the satisfaction of sheer smooth form to be found in early Chinese jade; and softer stones, such as amber and jet, could also be used to admirable effect for personal ornaments, as for instance the jet necklace or collar (no. 16). The arrangement of the beads and space-plates in such necklaces is known as a result of careful excavation in which the exact position of the elements of such a collar in a grave was noted: this precise record gave a new significance to a whole series of older finds and transformed them from a handful of miscellaneous beads into graceful pieces of jewellery.

Gold, almost entirely of Irish and Scottish origin, was extensively used from about 1600 B.C. in British jewellery, sometimes combined with amber but usually relying on the intrinsic beauty of the plain metal for its effect. We can see two main phases in the development of the goldsmith's craft in the second millennium; the first uses the relatively restricted supplies of metal to obtain the maximum effect by beating it into thin sheets. To this 'sheet' phase belong such objects as the thin gold collars or *lunulae* (no. 17), themselves copies of the crescentic necklaces of the type of no. 16; and in southern England we can perceive technical advances in metal-work which seem to be due to trade contacts with the Mycenaean world in the century about 1500–1400 B.C. The gold cup from a grave at Rillaton in Cornwall (nos. 10, 11) is a fine example of this remarkable link between the Aegean and the North—south-west England was then at the meeting of trade-routes from the Aegean, via central Europe and the western sea-ways, and from Ireland, and profited by both.[1]

Although the 'sheet' technique in gold-work was of course used throughout prehistory where the nature of the work demanded it (for instance in the more elaborate collars such as no. 21, or in great pieces of horse-trapping such as no. 27), we see, however, about 1000 B.C. the use of metal in 'bar' form, implying a greater command over the sources of the raw material, and used in such ornaments as the four-foot long coiled neck- or arm-ornament (no. 26). Here the cutting of the solid gold bar into four leaves is an imitation of soldered strip-work of the type known in the east Mediterranean about this time (and earlier): the technique of soldering was never achieved by the Irish Bronze Age gold-workers.

British gold-work was constantly developing under the stimulus of other schools of craftsmanship in Europe with which goldsmiths in these islands were brought into touch by their trade. In the later Irish Bronze Age, for instance, we can trace the influence of designs used by contemporary Scandinavian metal-workers, and the closely spaced, compass-drawn concentric circles seen for instance on the disk (no. 22) and along the gunwale of the boat-bowl (nos. 28, 29) are almost certainly derived from Denmark or south Sweden; and it is interesting to see that these patterns appear in Ireland just about the time of the first imported amber, a Danish product.

British bronze-work also developed to a high degree of competence, and Ireland led the way in the manufacture of the impressive great cauldrons of riveted bronze plates such as nos. 34, 35. The use of several plates, rather than a single sheet wrought into shape, was in fact due to ignorance on the part of the Irish bronze-smiths of the methods of hammering and annealing necessary for such work (although the process had been well known in the ancient centres of civilization for centuries), and the cauldrons are, in this respect, really a superb example of evading a technical difficulty, and the rivets are turned to good effect by being made a feature of the decoration.

Some rather remarkable pieces of wood-carving survive which are almost certainly of the Late Bronze Age. Of the shield (nos. 23, 24) and the boat-bowl (nos. 28, 29) there is no doubt, and the model boat with its shield-bearing

[1] *Proceedings of the Prehistoric Society*, IV (1938), 52 ff.

warriors (no. 30) has very good claims to be of the same date as the un-doubtedly Late Bronze Age circular shields of wood (nos. 23, 24) or those mounted with bronze (no. 25). The human figures (nos. 31–33) have, we admit, no direct evidence of date, but they are included at this point in our series for their intrinsic interest and in the hope that by drawing attention to them we may gain new information on their affinities: similar wooden figures are known from Brandenburg and Jutland. When found, the Ballachulish figure 'lay on its face, covered with a sort of wicker work; and several pole-like sticks lying near it suggested the idea that it might have been kept in a wattled hut'.[1] Whether images or idols, these figures are in their way among the most striking pieces of ancient British art.

When we turn to works of art in Britain from about the end of the third century B.C. until (and in some regions during) the Roman occupation of A.D. 43–400, we can for the first time in our survey consider them as a group, related to one another in a continuous stylistic sequence. It is convenient to call this art 'Celtic': its craftsmen and its patrons were linguistically Celts, and within the restricted scope of this book we are not concerned with the problems of what is, and what is not, to be called Celtic in post-Roman, early Christian art.

The origins of prehistoric Celtic art are to be found in the Rhineland and eastern France in the fifth century B.C., where three traditions were blended into something wholly new and distinctive: the old geometric art of the Euro-pean Bronze Age, ideas (notably fantastic animal ornament) from the Orient, probably through the Scyths, and, most important, certain motifs of classical Greek art, such as the palmette and the plant-tendril, acquired at second hand as a result of the wine trade with Etruscan Italy.[2]

In Britain the new art was introduced by trade and immigration from the second half of the third century B.C. onwards, and from the first we can see how it takes on a peculiarly characteristic insular form, developing parallel to the Continent in some respects, but with an individual genius of its own. It is an art which has survived almost entirely in metal-work, and it is the expression of the aristocratic element in a heroic society: the barbaric ostenta-tion of a warrior nobility finding an outlet in the magnificence of shields, scabbards, helmets and spears, in chariot trappings and in harness. The lavish hospitality of the chieftain shows itself in the decorated fire-dogs of the hearth,

---

[1] *Proceedings of the Society of Antiquaries of Scotland*, xv (1881), 158, with illustrations of the Brandenburg and Danish figures.

[2] P. Jacobsthal, *Early Celtic Art* (1944).

and the tankards for the feast; the vanity of the ladies of the court in the great chased bronze mirrors. Such a society was by its very nature doomed to destruction by the *pax Romana*. The impact on the native craftsmen of Roman provincial art was an influence deadening enough, but they had already lost their patrons with the extinction of the Celtic nobility, and a tradition based upon feudal magnificence and battle panoply could hardly survive in the new world of Roman Britain. Only in the north and in Ireland can we trace the later stages of Celtic art, on the fringes or beyond the bounds of the Roman province.

The main area of production of the metal-work under consideration (nos. 37–73) was an arc of country stretching from Somerset to Yorkshire, and it has a background of small peasant communities static in themselves, but linked by the travelling craftsmen and by the movements in warfare and raiding of the upper classes of the society: it is much the world of Homer or of Beowulf, and is in fact described in very similar terms in the more or less contemporary Irish stories of the Ulster Cycle.[1] The earliest pieces of metal-work we can identify are likely to belong to about 200 B.C., and most lie between about 150 B.C. and A.D. 30. Politically, the area was divided into tribes under princes or chieftains, and from 75 B.C. the newly arrived Belgae from the Continent established a powerful kingdom in south-eastern England, while in the north the recognition of the great tribe of the Brigantes as a client kingdom after the conquest of A.D. 43 led to their hegemony and prosperity until their inclusion in the Province after A.D. 71.

From the beginning, two regional schools of Celtic art can be identified, one in the north-east and the other in the south-west. What seem to be the earliest pieces belong to the northern and eastern provinces, either actually found there, such as the Witham scabbard-mount and shield (nos. 46, 56), or of north-eastern style, such as the Torrs horse-mask from south-west Scotland (nos. 38–40) and the helmet without location (no. 54). This early school uses plastic form, usually in cast or repoussé bronze, to great effect, sometimes combined with fine incised tendril motifs, and has from the first two modes, asymmetric and symmetrical, the latter usually based on the classical palmette motif. The Torrs horse-mask and the helmet (no. 54), and some elements of the shield (no. 56), show a symmetrical arrangement of pattern, but in the last piece asymmetry is also present in the detail, and is very well shown in the scabbard-mount (no. 46). (It also appears in engraved

---

[1] For the literary sources, cf. T. G. E. Powell, 'The Celtic settlement of Ireland', in *Early Cultures of North-West Europe* (Chadwick Memorial Studies, 1950), 173.

ornament on the Torrs horse-mask, though not in the photographs shown here.) The date of these pieces is probably between 250 and 150 B.C.[1]

It is convenient to follow the north-eastern style in its subsequent development before turning to that of the south-west; naturally there was give-and-take between the two provinces, and some pieces do indeed show a mixture of traditions. But in the north-eastern manner of a slightly later date is the helmet from the Thames at Waterloo Bridge (no. 53), with its thin relief tendril-ornament following an asymmetric pattern. This closely resembles a Yorkshire scabbard almost certainly about 75–50 B.C. (not illustrated), and to the same date is to be assigned the beautiful crescentic plaque from Llyn Cerrig (no. 42), which, although found in Anglesey, must have been made in some north-east English atelier. The asymmetric triquetral design of this plaque was used as the basis of a whole series of works in relief or engraving from both the north-eastern and the south-western areas, and indeed one of the striking characteristics of British Celtic art is the relatively limited number of basic motifs coupled with the most amazing fertility of inventive genius in their use.

The dagger-hilt in stylized human form (no. 37) is one of the rare surviving decorative works wrought in iron, rather than in bronze, and it copies continental forms introduced into Yorkshire a little before 100 B.C. The later development of the north-eastern style, in the middle of the first century A.D., is shown by the haunting horse's head (no. 59), a remarkable object found in a hoard of metal-work in the North Riding of Yorkshire near the great Stanwick earthworks, which may well have been the defences of a tribal capital: at all events the hoard is likely to date from the period of Brigantian prosperity between A.D. 43 and 71.

From Yorkshire the art-style of the north-eastern school was taken to Ireland, probably late in the first century B.C., with an invasion of warriors attested by archaeological remains and probably by literary traditions too. The magnificent gold neck ornament (no. 45) from Broighter, Co. Derry, shows a development of the style of relief work already seen on the Waterloo helmet (no. 53); and the bronze disks (nos. 48, 49) take the story of the peculiarly Irish development well into the period of the Roman occupation of Britain.

The final development of Celtic art on the fringes of the Roman province is represented by one of the finest pieces in our whole series, the bronze tankard from Trawsfynydd in North Wales (no. 73). The open-work pattern

---

[1] In general, our dates are in accordance with Sir Cyril Fox's studies listed in the footnote at the end of this essay, p. 11.

of the handle, with the junctions of the curves emphasized by little round bosses, relates it to other less splendid examples of the style from west Yorkshire and southern Scotland, especially on sword-scabbards which can be dated to the late first century A.D. Finally, the extraordinary bronze boar's head from Deskford in north-east Scotland (no. 61) is of the same or a rather later date, belonging to a local school best known by a series of baroque arm-rings, and ultimately related to the later north-eastern English style as shown in some of the pieces of the Stanwick hoard.

The south-west English style is best represented by a noble series of bronze mirrors with engraved backs, often of such proportions that they must have been held by a servant rather than by their user. The fine chased or incised patterns so characteristic of the south-western school do not, unfortunately, register well in photographs, but the mirror from Birdlip in Gloucestershire (no. 41) shows the superb balance of design which was achieved in these pieces. Stylistically it shows a stage of evolution in the pattern which should make it rather later than a mirror found in a grave at Colchester which can be dated to between A.D. 10 and 25: the Colchester mirror may have been a generation old when buried with its owner, and that from Birdlip (also from a grave) must at least date from the very beginning of the Christian era. The mounts from Chepstow and Sudeley (nos. 43, 44) show the Celtic craftsman at work upon minor pieces with the same sureness of touch as upon the great masterpieces; the little triangles of multi-coloured enamel on the Chepstow mount (no. 43) show the influence of Roman provincial enamelled objects in the first century A.D., and are quite foreign to the native tradition. We can see the same use of Roman enamelled devices still less satisfactorily on the Felmersham spout (no. 58).

The growth in power of the Belgic dynasties from the middle of the first century B.C. meant that south-eastern England was able to offer lucrative patronage to craftsmen skilled in making the traditional panoply of the Celtic courts. Talent was recruited from both the north-eastern and the south-western ateliers, and there are such pieces as the spear-head from the Thames (no. 47), which shows in its decorative plates the merging of two modes, north-eastern asymmetric motifs combined with the hatched 'basketry' technique used to form a background to the pattern in the south-western manner. The famous Battersea shield (no. 55) shows in its handling of relief-moulded circular elements a familiarity with the incised 'mirror-style'.

The blacksmith's craft is effectively shown in the great decorative fire-dogs with their terminals wrought as fantastic bulls' heads (nos. 50–52). Although many of these (including no. 50) have been found in Belgic princes' graves as part of the furnishings for a banquet in the other world, their craftsmanship is that of the west, somewhere not far from the iron of the Forest of Dean, and the strange baroque monster from Capel Garmon (nos. 51, 52) was found remote from any Belgic contacts.

Within the Belgic sphere, however, a notable contribution to Celtic art was the imaginative handling of naturalistic animal forms in other ways. Naturalism, as we have seen, formed no part of the older Celtic art tradition in this country, though the fantastic treatment of animals, and occasionally of human beings, had been known on the Continent since the fifth century B.C. But the British version of this *interpretatio celtica* had to wait for the appearance of Roman naturalistic art among the imports to the Belgic capitals in south-eastern England in the half-century before the conquest, and for the imitation of coinage current in the Roman world. The bronze boars (nos. 66, 67), the Felmersham bucket-mount and fountain-spout (nos. 57, 58) and the horses on the coins (nos. 62–65) show the Celtic rendering of animal forms; and the Welwyn mount (no. 70) and the faces on the coins (nos. 71, 72) show the Celtic approach to the human figure. The charming animals from Milber Down (nos. 68, 69) must appear in this context, though it is possible that they are in fact not of British manufacture. Nevertheless they show tendencies present in Britain: the brilliant simplification of the swimming duck and the exquisite realism of the roped stag show the Celtic artist's approach in its two most divergent aspects, both present for the brief period before their submergence beneath the tide of the dreary mediocrity of Roman provincial art.[1]

[1] The bibliography of prehistoric Celtic art in Britain is very large, but the main sources are: E. T. Leeds, *Celtic Ornament* (1933); P. Jacobsthal, *Early Celtic Art* (1944), and in *Burlington Magazine*, LXXV, 31; Hawkes and Corder, *Antiquaries Journal*, XX (1940), 346; Cyril Fox, *A Find of the Early Iron Age from Llyn Cerrig Bach* (1947); *Archaeologia Cambrensis*, 1945, 199; *ibid* 1948, 24; *Antiquaries Journal*, XXVII (1947), 1; *ibid.* XXVIII (1948), 123; Piggott, *Proceedings of the Prehistoric Society*, XVI (1950), 1.

EXPLANATORY LIST OF PHOTOGRAPHS

1. ENGRAVING, Upper Palaeolithic. On bone, 2 inches high, from Pin Hole Cave, Derbyshire. *British Museum*

This engraving of a masked human figure on the end of a piece of bone was found at the Pin Hole Cave, Cresswell Crags, in the Derbyshire hills. The whole bone is $8\frac{1}{2}$ inches long.

The figure probably represents a man engaged in some sort of hunting magic.

2–4. CARVINGS, *c.* 1800–1500 B.C. On stone, from New Grange and Loughcrew, Ireland.

These three designs are on the walls of two of the very fine collective tombs of east central Ireland. New Grange lies five miles west of Drogheda, and consists of a passage leading to a corbel-vaulted burial chamber with three side-chambers opening out of it, the whole set in a large round mound of earth and stones. No. 2 is a triple spiral on one of the walling stones of the north side-chamber at New Grange, while no. 4 is a design of spirals, concentric circles, lozenges and zigzag patterns on the upper end of one of the walling stones of the passage at New Grange. The scale of these carvings may be gauged from the fact that the walling stones at New Grange are from 5 to 8 feet in height, and that the whole composition of no. 4 occupies the top 2 feet of one of the walling stones.

There are twenty-one prehistoric collective tombs at Loughcrew, at the western end of County Meath. Cairn *T*—often known as the Tomb of Ollamh Fodhla—is the finest of this group; in plan it is like New Grange. No. 3 is a design of concentric half-ellipses and arcs on one of the stones of the right-hand side chamber of Cairn *T*.

All three designs are done by pecking, and the details of this technique can be seen clearly in the spirals of no. 3 and the zigzag chevrons of no. 4.

5, 6. HANDLED DRINKING-MUG, *c.* 1800–1700 B.C. Pottery, $5\frac{1}{4}$ inches high, from Fordham, Cambridgeshire. *Museum of Archaeology and Ethnology, Cambridge*

This sturdy and simple vessel of reddish ware with the surface enriched with incised lozenge motifs belongs to the Early Bronze Age, and is one of a small group of pottery drinking-mugs which imitate wooden prototypes. The base of the Fordham mug is decorated with circular and radial designs reminiscent of the growth-ring and crack patterns on a wooden tankard.

7. BEAKER or DRINKING-CUP, *c.* 1800–1700 B.C. Pottery, 7 inches high, from Eriswell, Suffolk.

Museum of Archaeology and Ethnology, Cambridge

Cups of this and allied types are characteristic of the British Early Bronze Age, and at least 700 are known from graves and settlements ranging from Kent to the Orkneys. The colour is a reddish brown, with carefully executed designs made by impressing a notched stamp into the clay before firing.

8, 9. BOWL, probably *c.* 1200 B.C. Pottery, 6 inches in diameter, from grave at Kilmartin, Argyllshire. *National Museum of Antiquities, Edinburgh*

A highly ornamented bowl of reddish ware seen from the side and below, and decorated with panels and zones of impressions from a wide-toothed comb, and by zigzags in 'false relief'. It is of a type common in Ireland and also occurring in west Scotland, and is of Middle Bronze Age date.

10, 11. HANDLED CUP, *c.* 1500 B.C. Gold, $3\frac{1}{4}$ inches high, from grave in cairn on Rillaton Moor, Cornwall. *British Museum*

This cup is unique in northern Europe in showing the use of Mycenaean gold-smiths' techniques on native metal work. The shape recalls British Early Bronze Age pottery cups (e.g. no. 7), but the strengthening of the thin gold by corrugation must have been inspired by such Greek work as the pair of gold cups from Shaft Grave IV at Mycenae. The Rillaton cup was found in a cist-grave with a bronze dagger of a type current in south-west England at a time when trade contacts with Mycenaean Greece via central Europe are known to have existed, and its date must therefore approximate to that of the Shaft Graves.

12–15. DECORATED CHALK CYLINDERS, *c.* 1800–1500 B.C. $3\frac{1}{2}$ inches high by 4 inches in diameter. Local chalk, from grave in barrow on Folkton Wold in the East Riding of Yorkshire.

British Museum

Three chalk cylinders were found with the skeleton of a child of five years old; the smallest touched its head and the other two its hips. The motifs used in the decoration include the 'owl', 'face' or '*oculi*' motif—not unlike the Chad motif of contemporary folk art—concentric circles within concentric-opposed horseshoe or spectacle marks, a four-pointed star, and filled-in lozenges and triangles. They are likely to have been 'idols' of some form and have Iberian affinities.

16. NECKLACE, *c.* 1450–1400 B.C. Jet or lignite, 9¼ inches across externally, from grave at Poltalloch, Argyllshire.

National Museum of Antiquities, Edinburgh

Such crescent-shaped jet necklaces, with the rows of beads held in position by perforated spacers, are characteristic of the north English and south Scottish Middle Bronze Age in its opening phase. The type seems to have originated in central Europe, in amber, and such necklaces appear as imports in southern England about 1500 B.C. as the result of extended trade contacts (cf. the Rillaton gold cup, nos. 10, 11). The north British necklaces seem likely to be copies in the locally available semi-precious substance, jet.

17. NECK ORNAMENT ('LUNULA'), *c.* 1450–1400 B.C. Gold, 8 inches across externally, from Ross, barony of Kilkenny West, Co. West Meath.

National Museum of Ireland, Dublin

The crescent-shaped necklaces, of the type of no. 16, were translated in Ireland into magnificent neck ornaments of thin gold sheet, but the curious arrangement of the delicately incised ornament shows the relationship in its reminiscences of the space-beads at the two ends of the necklace.

18. CARVED BALLS, of uncertain date but perhaps *c.* 1800–1400 B.C. Stone, averaging about 1½ to 3 inches in diameter, from various sites in north-east Scotland.

National Museum of Antiquities, Edinburgh

These curious objects are something of an archaeological puzzle, as they have all been stray finds. But good parallels to the simpler type with many knobs come from Late Neolithic sites (probably after 2000 B.C.) in Orkney, and certain of the more elaborate forms with fine engraved spirals or concentric circles recall the Folkton chalk cylinders (nos. 12–15) and so may be *c.* 1500 B.C. Their use is wholly unknown.

19. AXE-HAMMER, *c.* 1800–1500 B.C. Stone, 5½ inches long, from Chippenham, Cambridgeshire.

Museum of Archaeology and Ethnology, Cambridge

This fine perforated stone axe-hammer was found together with an ogival bronze dagger and a scrap of beaker pottery with the primary burial in a round barrow. It is made of a finely grained igneous rock, has a flattened oval butt end and a parallel-sided oval shaft hole. Such axe-hammers do not occur commonly in Britain but, when they do, date from the Early Bronze Age.

20. AXE-HEAD, *c.* 1800–1500 B.C. Stone, 7 inches long, from Histon, Cambridgeshire. *Museum of Archaeology and Ethnology, Cambridge*

This polished ceremonial stone axe-head is made of green jadeite, and was probably imported into England from Brittany. It is very thin and in form and section closely resembles the earliest flat copper axes of the Early Bronze Age. Indeed these axe-heads of precious stone may be stone copies of metal tools.

21. NECK ORNAMENT ('GORGET'), *c.* 900–600 B.C. Gold, 12 inches in maximum diameter; found by accident in a narrow fissure in the rocks at Glenisheen, Ballyvaughan, Co. Clare. *National Museum of Ireland, Dublin*

A massive gold neck ornament, consisting of a crescentic neck-piece terminating in two circular plates 3½ inches in diameter. The main crescentic part is decorated with plain embossed ridges alternating with small ridges covered with a twisted-cable pattern in repoussé, the whole scheme of decoration bounded on the inside and outside by a design of embossed knobs. The circular terminal plates are decorated with embossed knobs and concentric circles. This is the finest example yet found of the class of Irish prehistoric gold ornaments known as 'gorgets' which date from the Late Bronze Age.

22. DISK, *c.* 900–600 B.C. Gold, 4¾ inches in diameter; found in a bog in the townland of Lattoon, Ballyjamesduff, Co. Cavan. *National Museum of Ireland, Dublin*

A paper-thin ornament of gold, heavily ornamented (perhaps by pressing the gold plate into an embossed bronze matrix) with a small central boss surrounded by closely packed concentric embossed lines, in turn surrounded by panels of geometrical ornament, in which the main elements are concentric circles, triangles of opposed diagonal lines, and filled-in hour-glass figures of two triangles joined at their apexes. The composition of concentric circles and opposed triangles gives a design reminiscent of draughts, dice boxes, and backgammon boards; hence the phrase 'dice-box ornament' sometimes used to describe the ornament of this gold disk. The decoration of concentric bands is not continuous; it is broken across in one place (bottom left in the photograph) by a wedge-shaped insertion of linear zones of lines and cross-hatched triangles.

23, 24. SHIELD, sixth to fifth century B.C. Alder wood, 2 feet 2 inches in maximum diameter, from Annadale, Co. Leitrim. *National Museum of Ireland, Dublin*

Circular shields of this type seem to be derived from forms in use in the eastern Mediterranean in the seventh or eighth century B.C. and surviving examples are almost all of bronze, though there is another Irish example which is made of leather.

15

25. SHIELD, sixth to fifth century B.C. Bronze, 1 foot 6 inches in diameter, from Auchmaleddie, New Deer, Aberdeenshire.
National Museum of Antiquities, Edinburgh

Thin bronze shields, either for parade use or with a backing of leather or wood, are fairly frequent in the British Late Bronze Age and are closely related to those of the type of nos. 23, 24. The Auchmaleddie shield has an unusual serpentine pattern which recurs on another from Coveney Fen, Cambridgeshire.

26. TWISTED ORNAMENT, *c.* 1000 B.C. Gold, 4 feet in length, from Grunty Fen, near Cambridge.
Museum of Archaeology and Ethnology, Cambridge

This fine gold ornament is made of a square-section bar of gold grooved to form four leaves, and then twisted, except for the solid bar terminals. It was found together with three palstaves, characteristic of the Middle Bronze Age in southern England. When found the ornament was twisted in a spiral as in the present photograph; it may originally have been twisted in this way and served as an arm ornament —indeed it is generally referred to as the Grunty Fen armilla; but it may, on the other hand, have originally been a neck ornament.

27. BREAST-PIECE FOR A HORSE, *c.* 900–600 B.C. Gold, on copper, $3\frac{1}{2}$ feet long by $8\frac{1}{2}$ inches deep; found in a barrow at Mold, Flintshire.
British Museum

This object consists of thin gold plate embossed and mounted on copper plate; pieces of the copper lining can be seen at the sides. The embossed design is a rich one of circular bosses of two sizes, pointed ovals, square bosses, pyramidal rivet heads; the whole arranged in long bands separated by raised lines. It was at first thought to be a piece of human armour and has often been referred to as the Mold corslet. It is more likely to have been a peytrel or brunt for a pony, and would have been worn across the breast partly as armour, partly as a splendid decoration. The finders referred to coarse cloth which was thrown away together with gold fastening straps. The cloth may have been part of a fringe attached to the peytrel; there are holes in the edges which may have served to attach such a fringe.

28,29. BOWL IN THE FORM OF A BOAT, probably sixth century B.C. Oakwood carved and inlaid with gold leaf, 7 by $4\frac{1}{2}$ inches, from Caergwrle, Flintshire.
National Museum of Wales, Cardiff

This very remarkable object seems to represent a rowing boat with shields hung along the gunwales, oars below these, and below the oars the zigzag waves of the sea. At each end are a pair of 'eyes'. The fine compass-drawn concentric circles on the 'shields' show the influence of Scandinavian metal-work techniques on the Irish and north-west British metal-work in the Late Bronze Age from 600 B.C. onwards.

30. **MODEL BOAT WITH WARRIORS**, probably sixth century B.C. Pinewood, 20 inches long, from Roos Carr, Holderness.

Hull Museum

This striking model was formerly thought to be of the Viking Age, but comparative evidence strongly suggests a Late Bronze Age date. The boat has a prow in the form of an animal's head, originally with inlaid quartz eyes like the figures, who hold a circular shield (cf. the Late Bronze Age shield, no. 25). The Ballachulish figure (no. 33) has similar quartz eyes.

31–33. **HUMAN FIGURES**, perhaps about sixth century B.C. or later.

31, from Shercock, Co. Cavan. Wood, 3 feet 9 inches high.

National Museum of Ireland, Dublin

32, from Dagenham, Essex. Scots fir, 18 inches high.

Colchester and Essex Museum

33, from Ballachulish, Argyllshire. Oak, 5 feet high.

National Museum of Antiquities, Edinburgh

These curious figures seem to be approximately contemporary, and are comparable with the warriors in the Roos Carr model (no. 30). A date in the Late Bronze Age is therefore suggested, though direct evidence is lacking. The Shercock figure is the most accomplished, and shares with the Dagenham and Roos Carr models a socket for a separate penis. The Ballachulish figure has inlaid quartz eyes in the Roos Carr manner.

34, 35. **CAULDRON**, sixth to fourth century B.C. Bronze, 21 inches in diameter and 16 inches high; found in a bog at Montgomery, Castlederg, Co. Tyrone. *National Museum of Ireland, Dublin*

This bronze cauldron is built up of sheets of metal riveted together with conical rivets; the sheets comprise a base, and then there are four zones of riveted plates of which the uppermost is bent over to make a rim decorated with concentric rows of embossed points. Two ring handles of cast bronze are attached to the rim by ribbed moulded staples. This cauldron and others of similar and slightly differing types have been derived from types of metal bucket used in Italy and Austria in the first half of the first millennium B.C. There is now reliable evidence from associated finds, comparative archaeology, and pollen analysis to date this type of cauldron in western Britain to between 600 and 300 B.C.

36. **SHAFT-MOUNTING**, sixth to fifth century B.C. Bronze, $4\frac{1}{2}$ inches long, from Dunaverney, Co. Antrim. *British Museum*

This cylindrical mount ornamented with rings and bird figures forms part of the decoration of the wooden shaft of a pronged object of a class usually known as flesh-hooks, but possibly in fact used as goads (*stimuli*) for chariot-ponies. The charming birds are in the Hallstatt tradition of continental Europe.

37. **SWORD-HILT**, first or second century B.C. Iron, $5\frac{1}{4}$ inches long, probably from Yorkshire. *British Museum*

Sword-hilts of the so-called 'anthropoid' type are an evolution of the European Iron Age, and the finest example from England is almost certainly an import. The hilt illustrated, however, is probably a British production copying the continental type-form.

38–40. **PARADE-MASK FOR A HORSE**, late third to early second century B.C. Bronze, $10\frac{1}{2}$ inches long; horns $8\frac{3}{4}$ inches high, from Torrs, Kircudbrightshire. *National Museum of Antiquities, Edinburgh*

Towards the end of the third century B.C., a school of metal-workers in the La Tène tradition was established in north-eastern England, and developed an insular style of great originality. This fantastic parade-mask or chamfrain, though found in Galloway, is one of the finest surviving products of this school, with repoussé and incised ornament. It seems probable that the heavy horns, though from the same atelier as the mask, are a later addition replacing a lighter feature such as a panache of feathers, and they may themselves have originally served as drinking-horn mounts.

41. **ENGRAVED MIRROR**, early first century A.D. Bronze, $10\frac{3}{4}$ inches in maximum diameter, from Birdlip, Gloucestershire. *Gloucester Museum*

The main design covering the back of the mirror is an engraved pattern of symmetrical scroll work with areas of filled-in basket-work pattern. The handle is moulded and its curves decorated by ribbed lines. Above the junction of the handle is a moulded scroll. Inside the end loop of the handle is a single pair, and inside the applied scroll are three pairs, of circular red enamel settings. This mirror is a masterpiece of engraved curvilinear design, and is one of the finest achievements of the British Celtic artists in the centuries immediately before the Roman conquest.

42. **CRESCENTIC PLAQUE**, early to mid first century B.C. Bronze, 7 inches in diameter, from Llyn Cerrig Bach, Anglesey.

National Museum of Wales, Cardiff

This is an approximately circular bronze plaque which because of its eccentrically placed circular hole has a crescentic appearance. In the centre and below the hole is a roundel enclosing a triquetral design in relief. Five holes mark where studs were held. The original purpose of this plaque is uncertain. The opening is only $3\frac{3}{4}$ inches in diameter so that the plaque could not have been used as a neck ornament like the *lunulae* and gorgets (nos. 17 and 21).

43. **HARNESS MOUNT**, second half of the first century A.D. Bronze, $2\frac{1}{2}$ inches long, from Chepstow.

Privately owned

This bronze harness mount is in the form of an **S**-scroll with knobbed terminals and rectangular plates decorated with a double band of triangles attached to each side. The knobs and plates are decorated with red and yellow enamel. Each of the rectangular plates has a rectangular loop at the back and it is likely that the leather harness went through these loops. The decoration shows a combination of the free curves of La Tène art with the angular decoration which, with its use of coloured enamels, is due to the influence of Roman provincial art.

44. **ENAMELLED ORNAMENT**, first half of the first century A.D. Bronze, $3\frac{1}{2}$ inches across, found near Sudeley Castle, near Cheltenham.

Privately owned

This bronze ornament, possibly a horse-trapping, is a bold design of graceful eccentric curves incorporating as its main feature two sunken circles with bead margins, each enclosing a three-pointed geometrical lobate figure on a stippled ground. There are four sunken circular settings in each of the three pointed figures, and eight more in the marginal curves of the circles and the two open-work loops; all these settings would originally have held enamel, and traces of red enamel still survive in some of them.

45. **NECK ORNAMENT (TORC)**, first century B.C. Gold, 8 inches in inside diameter, from Broighter, Co. Derry.

National Museum of Ireland, Dublin

This magnificent neck ornament is based on a continental form of the third century B.C., but the engraved and repoussé decoration are characteristically later, and Irish. The 'snail-shell' relief spirals are quite distinctive, related to similar pattern on a Scottish gold ornament from Cairnmuir, and represent a local adaptation of incised linear spirals to plastic forms.

2-2

46. **SCABBARD-MOUNT,** late third to early second century B.C. Gilt bronze, 5¼ inches long, from the River Witham near Lincoln.

Duke of Northumberland's Collection, on loan to British Museum

A product of the same school as the Torrs horse-mask (nos. 38–40), this bronze mounting of a leather sword-scabbard shows a brilliant use of asymmetric ornament in plastic relief and line incision.

47. **DECORATED SPEAR-HEAD,** first century B.C. Iron with bronze plates, complete plate 3¾ inches long, from the River Thames, London. *British Museum*

The asymmetric (though balanced) ornament of the decorative bronze plates and their use of a formal hatched background to the incised designs suggest a combination of the two main art traditions in Iron Age Britain. The asymmetry belongs to the north-eastern school (cf. nos. 38–40, 46 above) but the hatched background or 'basketry' is characteristic of the south-west (cf. no. 41).

48, 49. **TWO DISKS,** probably second century A.D. Bronze, 9 inches in diameter, from Ireland. *British Museum*

These two photographs show (upper photograph, 48) a complete view, and (lower photograph, 49) a detail, of two bronze disks from Ireland decorated with repoussé scrolls. The general layout of the design is the same as the Llyn Cerrig Bach plaque (no. 42). A circular sunken area placed eccentrically in the nearly circular disk is surrounded by ornament in heavy relief, the main feature being the two flamboyant scroll patterns. While the ornament is essentially a geometrical fantasy it is difficult not to see a grotesque face behind the fantasy —the eyes represented by the scrolls and the open mouth by the sunken circle

50. **FIRE-DOG WITH OX-HEAD TERMINALS,** early first century A.D. Iron, 28 inches high, from Barton, Cambridgeshire.

Museum of Archaeology and Ethnology, Cambridge

Double-ended fire-dogs such as this stood in front of the open hearth, and in several of the graves of the Celtic nobility in south-east England provision for feasting with a guest in the after-world was made by depositing two such fire-dogs together with amphorae of wine, etc., with the dead.

51, 52. OX-HEAD TERMINAL OF A FIRE-DOG, first century B.C. to first century A.D. Iron, $9\frac{1}{2}$ inches high, from Capel Garmon, Denbighshire. *Private collection, on loan to National Museum of Wales, Cardiff*

Ox-head terminals are a usual feature of Celtic fire-dogs (cf. no. 50), but this shows a flamboyant and baroque rendering that is unique. To the stylized animal's head has been added a fantastic knobbed crest recalling that on a helmet. The whole conception has a bizarre and startling effect.

53. HELMET, first century B.C. Bronze, 8 inches in diameter at the base, $16\frac{3}{4}$ inches between the tips of the horns, found in the River Thames at Waterloo Bridge. *British Museum*

This fine bronze horned helmet is made of thin bronze plates riveted together to form a cap with two wide hollow pointed horns. The decorated strips of metal-work which cover the joins of the plates are secured by small pins or rivets set closely together giving a beaded effect. The centre area of the cap is decorated with three enamel studs surrounded by a design of slight, tenuous, but graceful curves in relief, and in a style related to the north-east English school of Celtic metal-work. The helmet was probably originally fastened to the head by chin-straps, but it should be noted that it is barely large enough to fit the head of an average modern man. It is probably a parade or ceremonial piece: certainly it is very thin and would only have afforded very slight protection in warfare.

54. HELMET, first century B.C. Bronze, $6\frac{3}{4}$ by $8\frac{3}{8}$ inches in diameter at the base, of uncertain provenance, but probably somewhere in the north of England. *British Museum*

This helmet originally had a knob on the summit for which rivet-holes remain. The broad flat decorated plate which gives the helmet the appearance of a modern jockey's cap is a neck-guard. These broad neck-guards are a feature of Roman helmets, which also had cheek pieces, as this helmet may also have had originally. The neck plate is decorated with a curvilinear geometrical pattern also incorporating, as does the Waterloo helmet, cross-scored disks for enamel, and is related stylistically to the Torrs horse-mask (nos. 38–40).

55. SHIELD, first century B.C. Gilt bronze with red enamel, 32 inches long, from the River Thames at Battersea. *British Museum*

This shield is a justly famous and almost hackneyed piece, but this should not blind us to its excellencies of design and craftsmanship. It has the characteristically

21

elongated outline of the Celtic shields in this country and on the Continent, and the symmetrical repoussé designs represent a development from those, for instance, on the Torrs horse-mask (no. 38). The enamel is set in *cloisons* to form swastika-shaped patterns.

56. SHIELD, late third to early second century B.C. Bronze, 44 inches long, from the River Witham near Lincoln. *British Museum*

A companion to the scabbard-mount from the same place (no. 46), this is the finest surviving shield in the early north-eastern style. The central boss and the terminal disks have ornament in repoussé and incised line, and the shield was further originally decorated with the applied figure of a highly stylized boar, now only faintly visible by discoloration and rivet-holes.

57. BUCKET-HANDLE MOUNT, first half of the first century A.D. Bronze, $1\frac{3}{4}$ inches between the tips of the horns, from Felmersham on Ouse, Bedfordshire. *British Museum*

This bucket-handle mount is modelled in the form of a cow's head curiously mixing realism and *naïveté*; the horns and ears are good, but the squinting eyes, done by a simple ring-and-dot technique, though animated, are unreal. But such realism as exists in the modelling is in contrast with much of the fantasy shown by other Belgic artists in Britain.

58. SPOUT IN THE FORM OF A FISH, first half of the first century A.D. Bronze, $2\frac{1}{2}$ inches from side to side, from Felmersham on Ouse, Bedfordshire. *British Museum*

A bronze spout in the form of a fish. In the eye-sockets are traces of something which may be enamel or some gum for fixing another inlay. The type of fish represented can be only a matter of guess-work: perhaps carp or tench. The crescentic plaque at the back is decorated with rather poor spirals in champlevé enamel.

59. MOUNT IN THE FORM OF A HORSE HEAD, mid first century A.D. Bronze, $3\frac{3}{4}$ inches long, from Stanwick, North Riding of Yorkshire. *British Museum*

A great hoard of Celtic metal-work was found about a century ago near a great complex of earthworks at Stanwick which may well represent a tribal centre. The hoard is likely to date from the heyday of the Brigantes, in whose territory it was deposited. This horse-head mount has a very individual character, but stylistically it recalls some north-east Scottish metal-work of rather later date.

60. **FIGURE OF A HORSE**, probably first century B.C. to early first century A.D. Turf cut on chalk hillside, 365 feet long, at Uffington, Berkshire.

The White Horse of Uffington was first recorded in the twelfth century A.D. and was for long considered a Saxon emblem cut by King Alfred after the Battle of Ashdown in 871. Stylistically, however, its affinities lie with the elongated representatives of animals in Celtic art, including those of horses on British coins, and it is therefore most likely to be of pre-Roman date.

61. **BOAR'S HEAD**, probably first century A.D. Bronze, 8½ inches long, from Deskford, Banffshire. *National Museum of Antiquities, Edinburgh*

The most likely explanation of this fine piece of Celtic art is that it formed part of a standard or ensign carried in procession or battle. The treatment of the eyes relates it to pieces from the Stanwick hoard (though not to that illustrated in no. 59), and a date probably late in the first century A.D. seems suitable.

62, 63. **COINS WITH PRANCING HORSES**, early first century A.D. Gold, approximately ½ inch in diameter, from Essex.
British Museum

These two coins were struck by Cunobelinus at Camulodunum (Colchester) and bear his abbreviated name. The horse is copied from a Roman coin prototype; and on no. 62, while very spirited, it is still in a fairly pure classical tradition. No. 63, however, shows the Celtic art styles mingling with the classical, producing a wilder and more exciting rendering of the same animal.

64. **COIN WITH HORSE**, early first century A.D. Gold, approximately ½ inch in diameter, from south-east England. *British Museum*

This coin of the Trinovantes tribe is derived from the same sources as nos. 62 and 63, but here the Celtic influence is stronger and the movement towards fantasy is taken a stage further.

65. **COIN WITH HORSE**, early first century A.D. Gold, approximately ½ inch in diameter, from south-west England. *British Museum*

Nos. 62–64 were coins of Belgic tribes in eastern Britain where Roman influences were strong, but this is of the Dobuni tribe, whose capital was at Cirencester. In the coins outside the Belgic series the horses become more schematized and purely Celtic in feeling, but the design becomes disintegrated and thin.

66, 67. **BRONZE FIGURES,** first century B.C. to first century A.D. Bronze, each about 3 inches in length, from Hounslow, Middlesex.
British Museum

The top figure of a boar can stand on its own legs; the lower figure has a perforated flange on its back which may have been for attaching it to some other object, perhaps a chariot, or standard or helmet. The purpose of both the figures is uncertain: they may have been toys or amulets or helmet crests. Leeds, in his *Celtic Ornament*, finds these figures, like all representations by the insular Celts of boars, very poor: 'The animal is at best a very sorry hog', he writes. We can agree that neither of the figures represented is realistic, but we find them, particularly no. 66, full of charm and interest. The head of no. 66 with its well-modelled snout and ears reveals a playful fantasy in Celtic art of a very different kind from the elaborate fantasies of so much of the decoration on metal-work.

68. **SWIMMING DUCK,** probably first century A.D. Bronze, 2½ inches long, from Milber Down Fort, south Devon.
Torquay Museum

This superbly stylized bird, holding a disk-shaped object in its mouth and with the conventionalized water ripples incised along its lower part, was found with no. 69 below and a naturalistic bird figure in excavations in the ditch of Milber Down Fort, stratified above pottery of the first century B.C.

69. **ROPED STAG,** probably first century A.D. Bronze, 2½ inches long, from Milber Down Fort, south Devon. *Torquay Museum*

A far more naturalistic rendering than no. 68 with which it was found, this small figure shows strong classical influence though retaining much Celtic feeling. The animal has been brought to the ground by a rope, seen round its neck and over one hind leg, and is choking. It is possible that either one or both of these bronzes may be imports from Gaul.

70. **MOUNT IN THE FORM OF A HUMAN HEAD,** early first century A.D. Bronze, 2 inches high, from burial at Welwyn, Hertfordshire.
British Museum

This little mount, one of three and here enlarged to twice its actual size, comes from a tomb provided with fire-dogs similar to no. 50, and other objects. It presents a brilliantly formalized version of the Celtic chieftain's face with combed-back hair and heavy moustache.

24

71, 72. HUMAN HEADS ON COINS, early first century A.D. Bronze, approximately ½ inch in diameter, from Biggleswade, Bedfordshire, and eastern England.   *British Museum*

Of these coins bearing heads probably of deities, no. 71 was minted at Verulamium (St Albans) by Tasciovanus, and no. 72 by his son Cunobelinus, who ruled from Camulodunum (Colchester) and whose abbreviated name appears on coins 62 and 63. The full beard of no. 71 is in contrast to the drooping moustache and 'imperial' of no. 72. In both coins the treatment is essentially Celtic and non-classical.

73. TANKARD, second half of the first century A.D. Bronze-plated wood, 5¾ inches high by 7 inches in diameter, from Trawsfynydd, Merionethshire.   *Liverpool Museum*

This tankard is built of wooden staves cased round with thin bronze plate turned down over the rim; the base is of wood. The top and bottom of the tankard have the same diameter; the sides are concave. The bronze handle consists of an open-work scroll design with **S**-curves, and is fixed top and bottom by plates consisting of pairs of roundels with central bosses. Apart from crescentic circles on the underside of the base, the only decoration is the handle. The vigour and simplicity of the handle, as well as the restraint in the decoration of the whole work, and its splendid craftsmanship and sense of balance, make it one of the finest achievements of La Tène art in western Europe.

LIST OF REFERENCES

PLATE

1   *Proceedings of the Prehistoric Society of East Anglia*, V (1926), 253; VI (1928), 27; Kendrick and Hawkes, *Archaeology in England and Wales*, 1914–31, 44–5; *Man* (1931), 117.

2–4   G. Coffey, *The Origins of Prehistoric Ornament in Ireland* (1897); *New Grange and Other Incised Tumuli in Ireland* (1912).

5, 6   C. Fox, *Archaeology of the Cambridge Region* (1923), plate II, 1; *Antiquity*, IX (1935), 348.

7   C. Fox, *Archaeology of the Cambridge Region* (1923), plate II, 2.

8, 9   Childe, *The Prehistory of Scotland* (1935), 90.

10, 11   *British Museum Quarterly*, CXCIII (1935), i.

12–15   W. Greenwell, *British Barrows* (1875), nos. lxx–lxxi; *Archaeologia*, LII, 14; British Museum, *Bronze Age Guide* (1920), 80–2; Elgee, *Archaeology of Yorkshire* (1933), 70–3.

16   *Proceedings of the Society of Antiquaries of Scotland*, LXIII (1929), 164; Childe, *Prehistory of Scotland* (1935), plate VIII.

17   E. C. R. Armstrong, *Catalogue of Irish Gold Ornaments* (1920), no. 33.

18   Childe, *Skara Brae* (1931), 100–8; *Proceedings of the Society of Antiquaries of Scotland*, XI (1875), 29, 313.

19   *Antiquaries Journal*, XV (1935), 62–3 and plate IX; *Cambridge Antiquarian Society* (1936), 134 ff.

20   *Proceedings of the Society of Antiquaries of Scotland*, LXXXIII (1950–1).

21   *Journal of the Royal Society of Antiquaries of Ireland* (1934), 138–9.

22   E. C. R. Armstrong, *Catalogue of Irish Gold Ornaments* (1920), 47; *Man* (1920), 45; *Proceedings of the Prehistoric Society* (1937), 371–2; R. A. S. Macalister, *The Archaeology of Ireland* (2nd ed., 1949), 196–8.

23, 24   *Proceedings of the Royal Irish Academy*, XXVII (c) (1909), 259.

25   Sprockhoff, *Handelgeschichte der Germ. Bronzezeit* (1930) 12.

26   *Proceedings of the Cambridge Antiquarian Society* (1906–7), 96–105; *Proceedings of the Society of Antiquaries of London* (1911–12), 39–49; C. Fox, *Archaeology of the Cambridge Region* (1923), 51–63.

27   *Archaeologia*, XXVI (1836), 422–31; British Museum, *Bronze Age Guide*, 93–4; Wheeler, *Prehistoric and Roman Wales*, 175–9; Grimes, *Guide to the Collections Illustrating the Prehistory of Wales* (1939), 84–5.

28, 29   Grimes, *Guide to the Collections Illustrating the Prehistory of Wales* (1939), 83.

30   Elgee, *Archaeology of Yorkshire* (1933), plate X; *Acta Archaeologica*, XIII (1942), 235.

REFERENCES

PLATE

31 Macalister, *Ancient Ireland* (1935), fig. 22.

32 *Transactions of the Essex Archaeological Society*, new series, XVI (1923), 288.

33 *Proceedings of the Society of Antiquaries of Scotland*, XV (1880–1), 158.

34, 35 *Archaeologia*, LXXX (1930), 1 ff.; *Antiquaries Journal* (1939), 367 ff.

36 British Museum, *Bronze Age Guide* (1920), 104.

37 British Museum, *Early Iron Age Guide* (1925), fig. 58, 3; *Proceedings of the Prehistoric Society*, XVI (1950).

38–40 Childe, *Prehistory of Scotland* (1935), 252 and plate I.

41 *Archaeologia*, LXI (1909), 331–3; E. T. Leeds, *Celtic Ornament*, 28–30; *Antiquaries Journal*, XXVIII (1948), 123–37; *Proceedings of the Prehistoric Society* (1949), 188–90.

42 Fox, *A Find of the Early Iron Age from Llyn Cerrig Bach, Anglesey* (Cardiff, 1947); *Archaeologia Cambrensis* (1945), 199–200.

43 *Archaeologia Cambrensis* (1932), 393; E. T. Leeds, *Celtic Ornament* (1933), 98; Grimes, *Guide to the Collections illustrating the Prehistory of Wales* (1939), 197.

44 *Antiquaries Journal* (1938), 76–7.

45 *Archaeologia*, LV, 391 and plate XXII.

46 *Antiquaries Journal*, XIX (1939), 194.

47 *Proceedings of the Prehistoric Society*, V (1939), plate XX.

48, 49 British Museum, *Early Iron Age Guide* (1925), 161.

50 Fox, *Archaeology of the Cambridge Region* (1923), 100; *Antiquity*, XXII (1948), 21.

51, 52 *Antiquaries Journal*, XIX (1939), 194.

53, 54 British Museum, *Early Iron Age Guide* (1925), 72, 107; C. E. Vulliamy, *Archaeology of Middlesex and London* (1930), 127–8; E. T. Leeds, *Celtic Ornament* (1933), 24, 26–7.

55, 56 British Museum, *Early Iron Age Guide* (1925), 106.

57, 58 *Antiquaries Journal*, XXIX (1949), 37 ff.

59 *Archaeologia*, LX (1906), 289.

60 M. Marples, *White Horses and Other Hill-Figures* (1949), 28.

61 J. Anderson, *Scotland in Pagan Times: The Iron Age* (1883), 117.

62–65 *Archaeologia*, XC (1944), 1–46.

66, 67 *Proceedings of the Society of Antiquaries*, II (III) (1864–7), 90; C. E. Vulliamy, *Archaeology of Middlesex and London* (1930), 134; British Museum, *Early Iron Age Guide* (1925), 147–8; E. T. Leeds, *Celtic Ornament* (1933), 95.

68, 69 *Devon Archaeological Exploration Society Proceedings* (1937), 6.

70 British Museum, *Early Iron Age Guide* (1925), 132.

71, 72 *Archaeologia*, XC (1944), 3–46.

73 Wheeler, *Prehistoric and Roman Wales*, 210–11; E. T. Leeds, *Celtic Ornament* (1933), 153–4; Grimes, *Guide to the Collections Illustrating the Prehistory of Wales* (1939), 196.

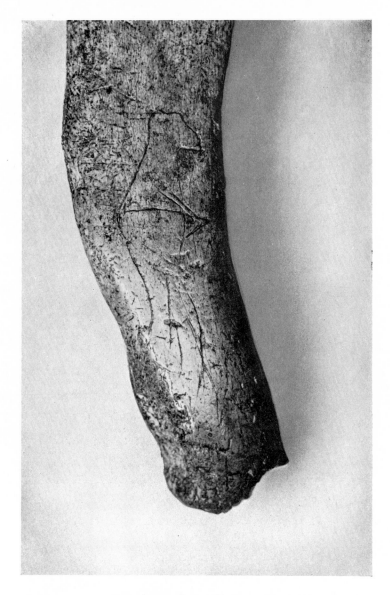

1. ENGRAVING on bone, from Pin Hole Cave, Derbyshire.
Upper Palaeolithic

2, 3. CARVINGS on stone, from New Grange and Loughcrew, Ireland.
c. 1800–1500 B.C.

4. CARVING on stone, from New Grange, Ireland. *c.* 1800–1500 B.C.

5, 6. HANDLED DRINKING-MUG, from Fordham, Cambridgeshire.
c. 1800–1700 B.C.

7. BEAKER, from Eriswell, Suffolk. *c.* 1800–1700 B.C.

8, 9. BOWL, from Kilmartin, Argyllshire. Probably *c.* 1200 B.C.

10, 11. HANDLED CUP, from Rillaton Moor, Cornwall. *c.* 1500 B.C.

12, 13. DECORATED CHALK CYLINDERS, from Folkton Wold, Yorkshire.
c. 1800–1500 B.C.

14, 15. DECORATED CHALK CYLINDERS, from Folkton Wold, Yorkshire.
c. 1800–1500 B.C.

16. NECKLACE, from Poltalloch, Argyllshire. *c.* 1450–1400 B.C.

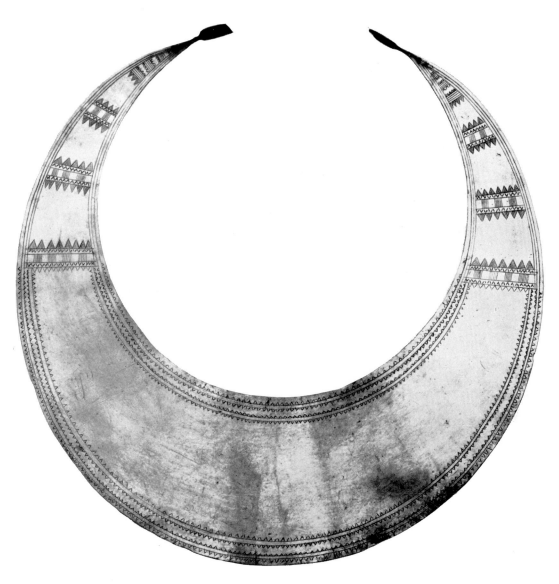

17. NECK ORNAMENT, from Ross, Co. Meath. *c.* 1450–1400 B.C.

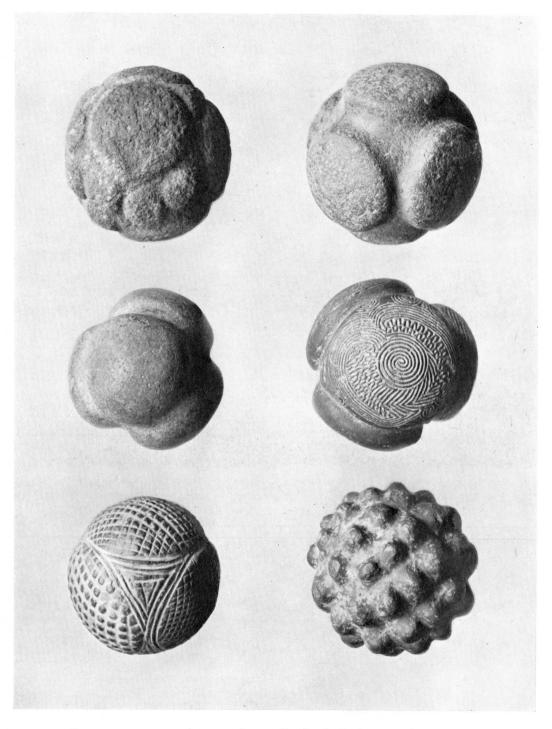

18. CARVED BALLS from north-east Scotland. Perhaps *c.* 1800–1400 B.C.

19. AXE-HAMMER, from Chippenham, Cambridgeshire. *c.* 1800–1500 B.C.
20. AXE-HEAD, from Histon, Cambridgeshire. *c.* 1800–1500 B.C.

21. NECK ORNAMENT, from Glenisheen, Co. Clare. *c.* 900–600 B.C.

22. DISK, from Lattoon, Co. Cavan. *c.* 900–600 B.C.

23, 24. SHIELD, from Annadale, Co. Leitrim. Sixth to fifth century B.C.

25. SHIELD, from Auchmaleddie, Aberdeenshire. Sixth to fifth century B.C.

26. TWISTED ORNAMENT, from Grunty Fen, near Cambridge. *c.* 1000 B.C.

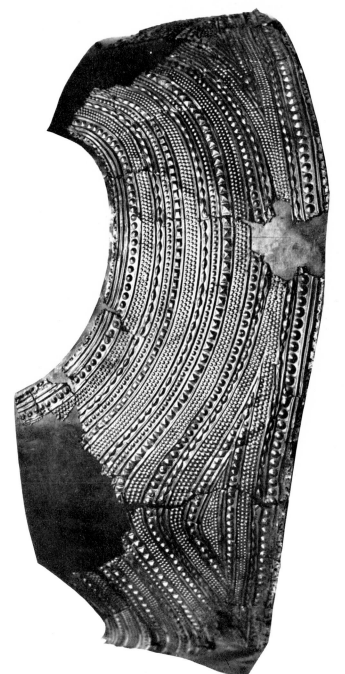

27. BREAST-PIECE FOR A HORSE, from Mold, Flintshire. c. 900–600 B.C.

28. BOWL IN THE FORM OF A BOAT, from Caergwrle, Flintshire.
Probably sixth century B.C.

29. BOWL IN THE FORM OF A BOAT.
(View of the under surface of no. 28 opposite)

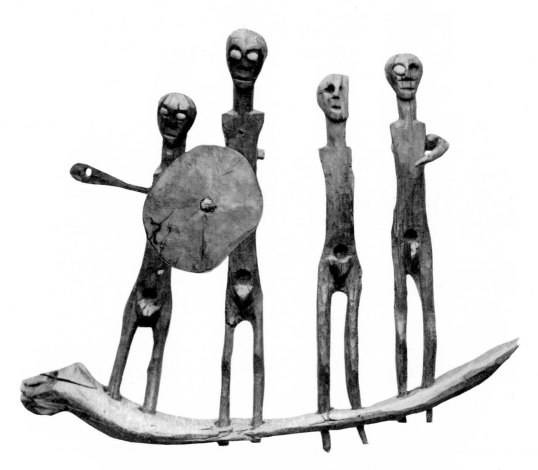

30. MODEL BOAT WITH WARRIORS, from Roos Carr, Holderness.
Probably sixth century B.C.

31, 32, 33. HUMAN FIGURES, from Shercock, Co. Cavan (left), from Dagenham, Essex (centre), and from Ballachulish, Argyllshire (right). Perhaps sixth century B.C. or later

34, 35. CAULDRON, from Montgomery, Co. Tyrone.
Sixth to fourth century B.C.

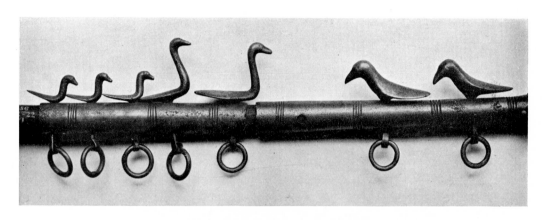

36. SHAFT-MOUNTING, from Dunaverney, Co. Antrim.
Sixth to fifth century B.C.

37. SWORD-HILT, probably from Yorkshire. First or second century B.C.

38. PARADE-MASK FOR A HORSE, from Torrs, Kircudbrightshire.
Late third to early second century B.C.

39. DETAIL OF PARADE-MASK (38)

40. DETAIL OF PARADE-MASK (38)

41. ENGRAVED MIRROR, from Birdlip, Gloucestershire. Early first century A.D.

42. CRESCENTIC PLAQUE, from Llyn Cerrig Bach, Anglesey.
Early to mid first century B.C.

43. HARNESS MOUNT, from Chepstow. Second half of the first century A.D.

44. ENAMELLED ORNAMENT, from near Cheltenham.
First half of the first century A.D.

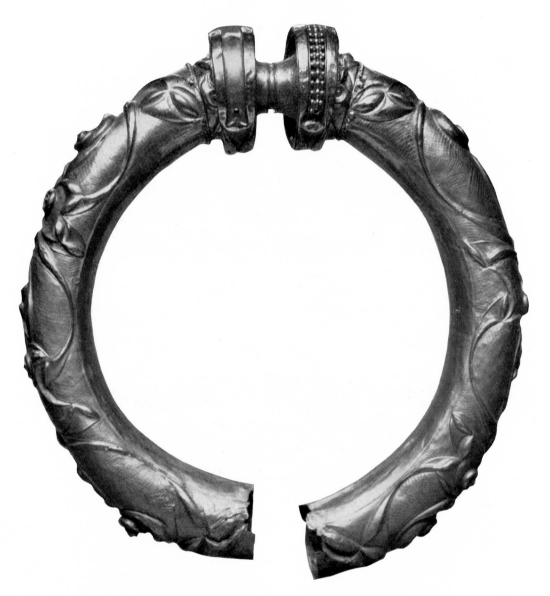

45. NECK ORNAMENT, from Broighter, Co. Derry. First century B.C.

46. SCABBARD-MOUNT, from the River Witham near Lincoln. Late third
to early second century B.C.

47. DECORATED SPEAR-HEAD, from the River Thames, London.
First century B.C.

48, 49. TWO DISKS, from Ireland. Probably second century A.D.

50. FIRE-DOG WITH OX-HEAD TERMINALS, from Barton, Cambridgeshire.
Early first century A.D.

51. OX-HEAD TERMINAL OF A FIRE-DOG, from Capel Garmon, Denbighshire.
First century B.C. to first century A.D.

52. OX-HEAD TERMINAL. (Side view of no. 51 opposite.)

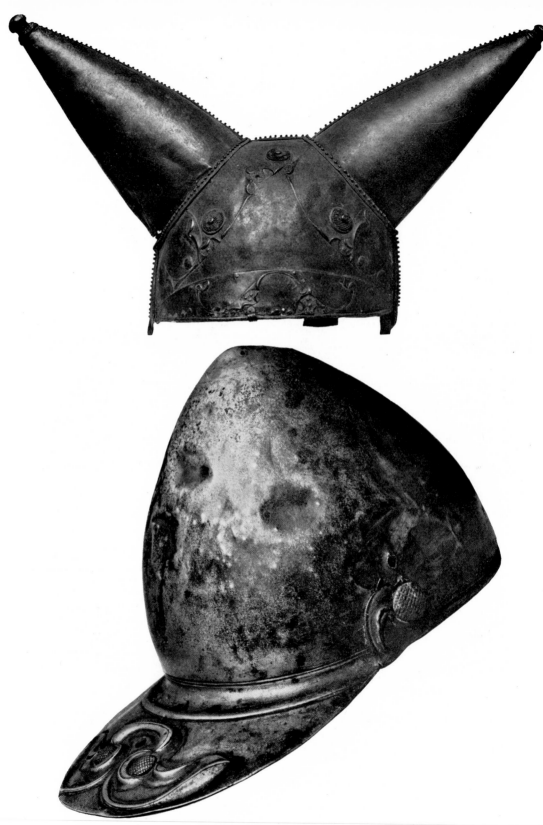

53. HELMET, from the River Thames. First century B.C.
54. HELMET, probably from the north of England. First century B.C.

55. SHIELD, from the River Thames.
First century B.C.

56. SHIELD, from the River Witham
near Lincoln. Late third to early
second century B.C.

57. BUCKET-HANDLE MOUNT, from Felmersham on Ouse, Bedfordshire.
First half of the first century A.D.

58. SPOUT IN THE FORM OF A FISH, from Felmersham on Ouse, Bedfordshire.
First half of the first century A.D.

59. MOUNT IN THE FORM OF A HORSE HEAD, from Stanwick,
Yorkshire. Mid first century A.D.

60. FIGURE OF A HORSE at Uffington, Berkshire. Probably first century B.C. to early first century A.D.

61. BOAR'S HEAD, from Deskford, Banffshire. Probably first century A.D.

Above

62, 63. COINS WITH PRANCING HORSES, from Essex. Early first century A.D.

Below

64. COIN WITH HORSE, from south-east England. Early first century A.D.

65. COIN WITH HORSE, from south-west England. Early first century A.D.

66, 67. BRONZE FIGURES, from Hounslow, Middlesex. First century B.C. to first century A.D.

68. SWIMMING DUCK, from Milber Down Fort, Devon. Probably first
century A.D.

69. ROPED STAG, from Milber Down Fort, Devon. Probably first century A.D.

70. MOUNT IN THE FORM OF A HUMAN HEAD, from Welwyn, Hertfordshire.
Early first century A.D.

71, 72. HUMAN HEADS ON COINS, from Biggleswade, Bedfordshire, and eastern England. Early first century A.D.

73. TANKARD, from Trawsfynydd, Merionethshire. Second half of the first century A.D.